Blue and Yellow in Summer

Bonnie Carole

rourkeeducationalmedia.com

Teaching Focus:

Ending Punctuation- Have students locate the ending punctuation for sentences in the book. Count how many times a period, question mark, or exclamation point is used. Which one is used the most? What is the purpose for each ending punctuation mark? Practice reading these sentences with appropriate expression.

Before Reading:

Building Academic Vocabulary and Background Knowledge

Before reading a book, it is important to set the stage for your child or student by using pre-reading strategies. This will help them develop their vocabulary, increase their reading comprehension, and make connections across the curriculum.

1. Read the title and look at the cover. *Let's make predictions about what this book will be about.*
2. Take a picture walk by talking about the pictures/photographs in the book. Implant the vocabulary as you take the picture walk. Be sure to talk about the text features such as headings, Table of Contents, glossary, bolded words, captions, charts/diagrams, or Index.
3. Have students read the first page of text with you then have students read the remaining text.
4. Strategy Talk – use to assist students while reading.
   - Get your mouth ready
   - Look at the picture
   - Think…does it make sense
   - Think…does it look right
   - Think…does it sound right
   - Chunk it – by looking for a part you know
5. Read it again.
6. After reading the book complete the activities below.

High Frequency Words

Flip through the book and locate how many times the high frequency words were used.

blue
color
is
it's
or
summer
the
they're
what
yellow

After Reading:

Comprehension and Extension Activity

After reading the book, work on the following questions with your child or students in order to check their level of reading comprehension and content mastery.

1. *Why do you need to eat a popsicle quickly during the summer months?* (Inferring)
2. *Why do people go camping in the summer instead of the winter?* (Asking questions)
3. *What is the weather like in the summer?* (Summarize)
4. *What activities do you like to do in the summer?* (Text to self connection)

Extension Activity

Bottle the ocean! With the help of a parent or teacher, you can have your own piece of summer all year round. You will need a clear, plastic water bottle, water, blue food coloring, sand, sea shells, glitter, and hot glue. Pour sand in the bottom of the bottle and add the seashells. Fill up the bottle with water making sure to leave room at the top. Add a few drops of blue food coloring and some glitter. Glue the cap to the bottle and shake. How many seashells are in your ocean? You can add sea creatures to the outside of the bottle with markers or stickers.

Which season is hot, bright, and filled with sun? You play outside and have tons of fun.

Do you need a clue? Summer is filled with **yellow** and **blue**!

Blue or yellow? What color is the ocean?

It's **blue!**

Blue or yellow? What color are the sails?

They're yellow!

Blue or yellow? What color is the Sun?

It's yellow!

Blue or yellow? What color is the bike?

It's **blue**!

Blue or yellow? What color are the birds?

They're yellow!

Blue or yellow? What color is the popsicle?

15

It's **blue!**

Blue or yellow? What color is the lemonade?

It's yellow!

Blue or yellow? What color is the tent?

It's **blue**!

Blue or yellow? What color is the bucket?

It's yellow!

Summer is the time for fun!

Index

Websites

http://www.eduplace.com/kids/hmsc/activities/simulations/grk/unitd.html

http://pbskids.org/sesame/games/color-me-hungry/

http://www.turtlediary.com/preschool-games/puzzle-games/color-factory.html

Meet The Author!
www.meetREMauthors.com

About the Author

Bonnie Carole lives in Illinois with her family. During the summer they enjoy going to the beach and drinking fresh, sour lemonade.

PHOTO CREDITS: Cover type © BlueRingMedia, cover photo © Volker Rauch; title ice pop © mikeledray; page 3 © Sergey Novikov; page 4-5 and 6 © karelnoppe; page 7 and 8 © Anson0618; page 9 and 10 © Elenamiv; page 11 park photo © zhangyang13576997233, bicycle photo © Gemenacom; page 12 © Gemenacom; page 13 and 14 © Tania Thomson; page 15 © sonya etchison, popsicle © L Barnwell; page 16 © L Barnwell; page 17 and 18 © Rob Marmion; page 19 and 20 © Tischenko Irina; page 21 and 22 © Christopher Elwell; page 23 © Studio 1One

Edited by: Luana Mitten

Cover design and Interior design: by Nicola Stratford
www.nicolastratford.com

Library of Congress PCN Data

Blue and Yellow in Summer/ Bonnie Carole
(Concepts)
ISBN 978-1-63430-049-0 (hard cover)
ISBN 978-1-63430-079-7 (soft cover)
ISBN 978-1-63430-107-7 (e-Book)
Library of Congress Control Number: 2014955460

Rourke Educational Media
Printed in the United States of America, North Mankato, Minnesota

Also Available as: